NOAH'S ARK

TERESA BATEMAN

Illustrated by **LAURA HULISKA-BEITH**

Highlights Press
Honesdale, Pennsylvania

2

ong ago there lived a righteous man named Noah. He and his wife had three sons—Shem, Ham, and Japheth. His sons had wives as well.

Noah tried to be a good neighbor, but lived in a time when people were hard-hearted and unkind, caring only for themselves and not for others. They no longer followed the laws they had been given, nor did they have any desire to change for the better.

Noah tried to teach them. He tried to warn them. He tried to help them change, but they would not listen. This made Noah very sad.

God was also sad. He warned Noah that a great flood of rain was coming, and commanded him to build an ark—a giant boat that would carry unusual cargo.

"But I don't know how to build an ark!" Noah exclaimed.

"Just do your best, and I'll do the rest," God promised.

5

So Noah started building. "Rain's coming. Best to be prepared," he told the neighbors who came to gawk as the ark loomed high overhead.

They laughed at him and didn't believe his words, but Noah worked on.

8

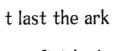

At last the ark was finished. It was beautiful and large, smelling of fresh wood and gleaming in the sunlight.

od told Noah to gather two of every kind of animal to put in the ark when the floods came, saving them along with his family.

"How shall I gather so many animals?" he asked.

"Just do your best, and I'll do the rest," God promised. And they came.

Noah and his family gathered all that they could, and other animals journeyed to join them. Soon the area around the ark was crowded with fur and feathers, scales and shells.

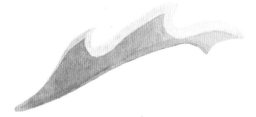

A single drop of rain settled into the dust nearby.

Dark clouds gathered overhead.

The giraffes towered.

The elephants swayed.

The monkeys chittered.

The donkeys brayed.

The hummingbirds hummed,

and the lizards crept.

The tigers purred,

and the leopards leapt.

The baboons played,

and the lions roared

as Noah cried out, "All aboard!"

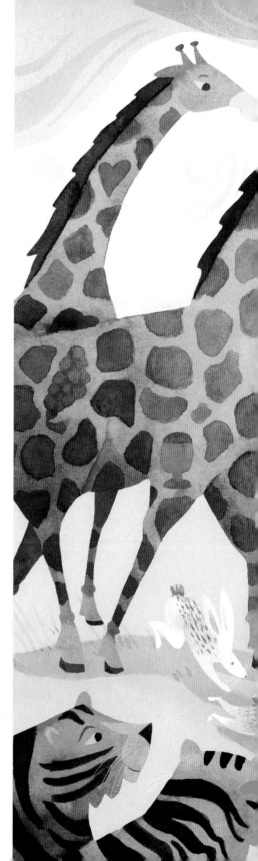

Noah and his family finished loading the last of the supplies and hurried into the ark after the animals. God closed the door behind them.

Soon the rain began falling harder, then it began to pour. Gradually the ark shifted, then it lifted and bobbed in the waves. Still the rain fell, and the waters rose, and all that was on the earth was swept away, except those who were with Noah.

or forty days and forty nights the rain continued. When it finally stopped, Noah looked out, and all he could see was water. The ark floated on, carried by the currents with its precious cargo safe within wooden walls. For one hundred and fifty days the ark went where the waters took it.

At last the waters began to recede, but Noah wondered if there would be a place for his family and the animals they cared for. So he opened a window and sent out a dove. It flew over the water but could find no place to rest, and returned to the ark.

They waited.

A week later, Noah opened the window again and sent the dove out once more.

They waited.

This time the dove returned with an olive leaf. She had found a tree! Noah understood there was a world out there to return to, but it was not ready for them yet. The water had not receded enough.

They waited.

 even days later,
Noah sent out
the dove again,
and this time she did not return.
She had found a place where she
could live, free of the water.

24

he ark came to rest on the top of a mountain. Noah flung open the door.

The giraffes towered.

The elephants swayed.

The monkeys chittered.

The donkeys brayed.

The hummingbirds hummed,

and the lizards crept.

The tigers purred,

and the leopards leapt.

The baboons played,

and the people cried

with joy and hope as they rushed outside.

25

Noah and his family looked at a world made new again.

"I don't know how to build a new world," Noah whispered.

"Just do your best, and I'll do the rest," God said. Then He placed a rainbow in the sky.

He told Noah, "This is my promise. By this sign you shall know that there will never be another flood such as this again."

The rainbow swept across the heavens. It was a symbol of love. It was a symbol of hope. It was God's promise.

It still is.

DEAR READER,

Every illustration in this book is also a Hidden Pictures puzzle. The picture clues around the text on each page can help you find the objects hidden in the illustration. If you are having trouble finding an object, here are a few tips:

- Look for objects that may be hidden in plain sight, disguised to look like something else.
- Try turning the book on its side to study the picture from a different angle.
- Try looking in an area where you haven't found anything yet.

PAGE 1

CAN YOU FIND:
- seal
- seahorse
- key
- oar
- pitcher
- lightning bolt
- loaf of bread
- canoe
- star
- fish hook
- paintbrush
- broccoli

PAGES 2-3

CAN YOU FIND:
- tortoise
- comb
- sailboat
- mushroom
- pineapple
- ax
- slice of bread
- bucket
- heart
- leaf
- peanut
- bell

PAGES 4-5

CAN YOU FIND:
- wishbone
- ball of yarn
- lemon
- pepper
- carrot
- seashell
- acorn
- dove
- saw
- spool of thread
- lightning bolt
- crown

PAGES 6-7

CAN YOU FIND:
- snail
- banana
- ruler
- pencil
- horn
- seal
- palm tree
- rose
- scissors
- snake
- ring
- fork

PAGES 8-9

CAN YOU FIND:
- rabbit
- jellyfish
- cherries
- apple core
- spool of thread
- mouse
- music pipes
- birdcage
- hummingbird
- trowel
- chisel
- sundial

PAGES 10-11

CAN YOU FIND:
- wave
- broom
- wedge of lemon
- corn cob
- seashell
- music note
- raindrop
- bow and arrow
- clover
- handbell
- candle
- pear

PAGES 12-13

CAN YOU FIND:
- rope
- fingerprint
- sickle
- spoon
- heart
- flower
- bunch of grapes
- goblet
- bucket
- hoe
- pine tree
- bowl

PAGES 14-15

CAN YOU FIND:
- needle
- fishhook
- pennant
- comb
- horn
- coin
- boot
- pawprint
- teapot
- olive
- star
- treble clef

PAGES 16-17

CAN YOU FIND:
- question mark
- bowl
- mug
- ladder
- pear
- ax
- mountains
- pitcher
- music note
- horn
- crescent moon
- tooth

PAGES 18-19

CAN YOU FIND:
- tack
- peapod
- fork
- lyre
- crown
- frying pan
- boomerang
- scarf
- hourglass
- open book
- cactus
- stool

PAGES 20-21

CAN YOU FIND:
- conch shell
- tulip
- ladle
- banana
- treble clef
- ruler
- wedge of lemon
- flute
- pennant
- key
- vase
- apple

31

PAGES 22-23

CAN YOU FIND:

- snake
- goblet
- rolling pin
- loaf of bread
- heart
- artist's brush
- bone
- wedge of lime
- whale
- horn
- fan
- drum

PAGES 24-25

CAN YOU FIND:

- slice of bread
- feather
- leaf
- crescent moon
- needle
- egg
- pennant
- plate
- mushroom
- twig
- pinecone
- pickle

PAGES 26-27

CAN YOU FIND:

- snail shell
- bone
- tooth
- pineapple
- crown
- radish
- horn
- crescent moon
- hand mirror
- carrot
- canoe
- mug

PAGES 28-29

CAN YOU FIND:

- candle
- diamond
- basket
- strawberry
- music note
- anchor
- vase
- bell
- acorn
- olive
- fried egg
- wheel

For Alex—child of love, hope, and promise.
—TB

Moon Firefly font copyright © by Annie Sauvage via Creative Market

For information about permission to reprint selections from this book,
please contact permissions@highlights.com.

Published by Highlights Press
815 Church Street
Honesdale, Pennsylvania 18431
Manufactured in Heshan, Guangdong, China
ISBN: 978-1-64472-118-6
Library of Congress Control Number: 2020943295
Mfg. 10/2020
First edition
Visit our website at Highlights.com.
10 9 8 7 6 5 4 3 2 1

Designed by Amy De Lay
The text is set in Sunshine.
The illustrations were painted in watercolor and digitally enhanced.